Adult Coloring book Day of the Dead & Mardi Gras

Vol 3

I0468151

By: L. M. Boelz

pages

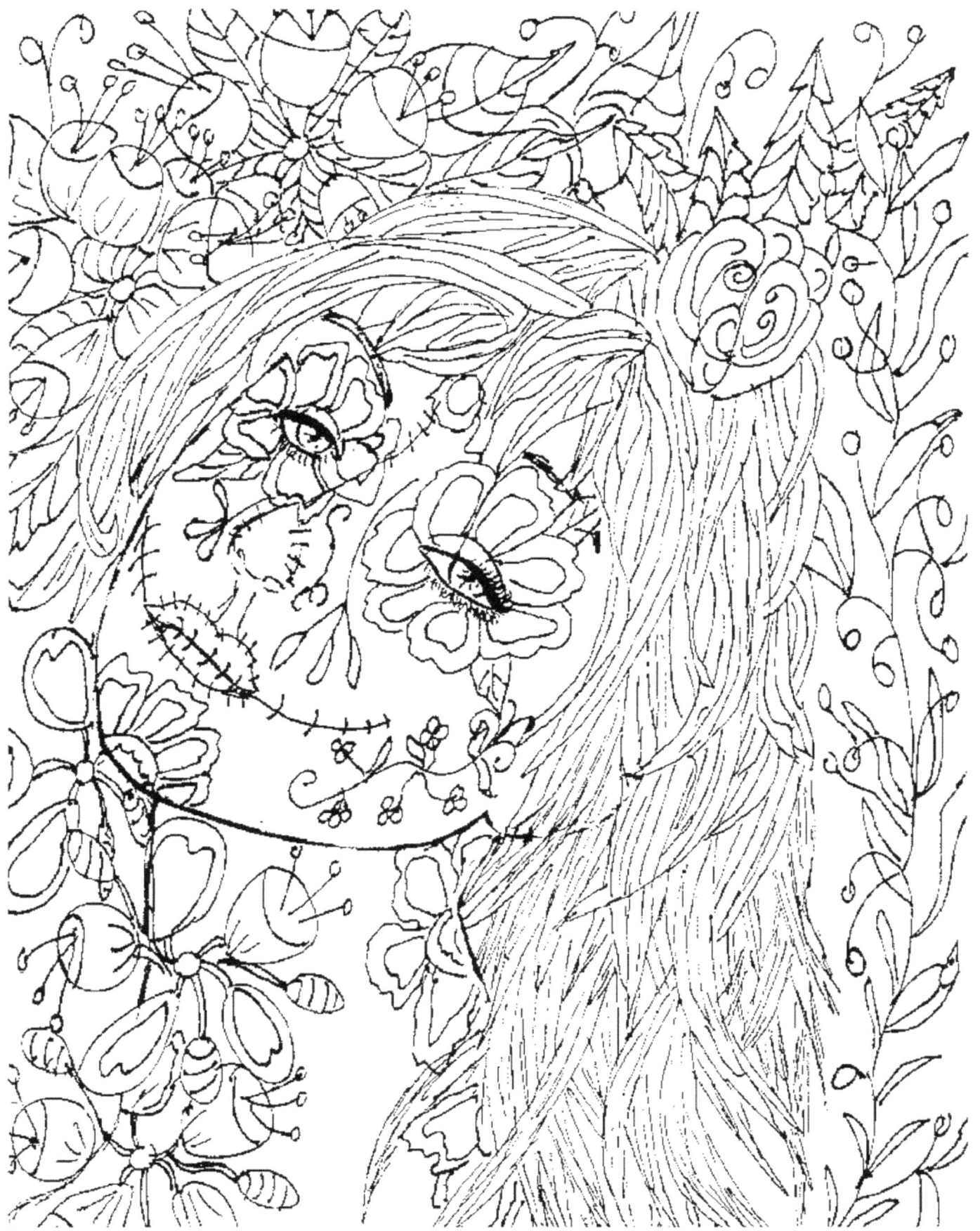

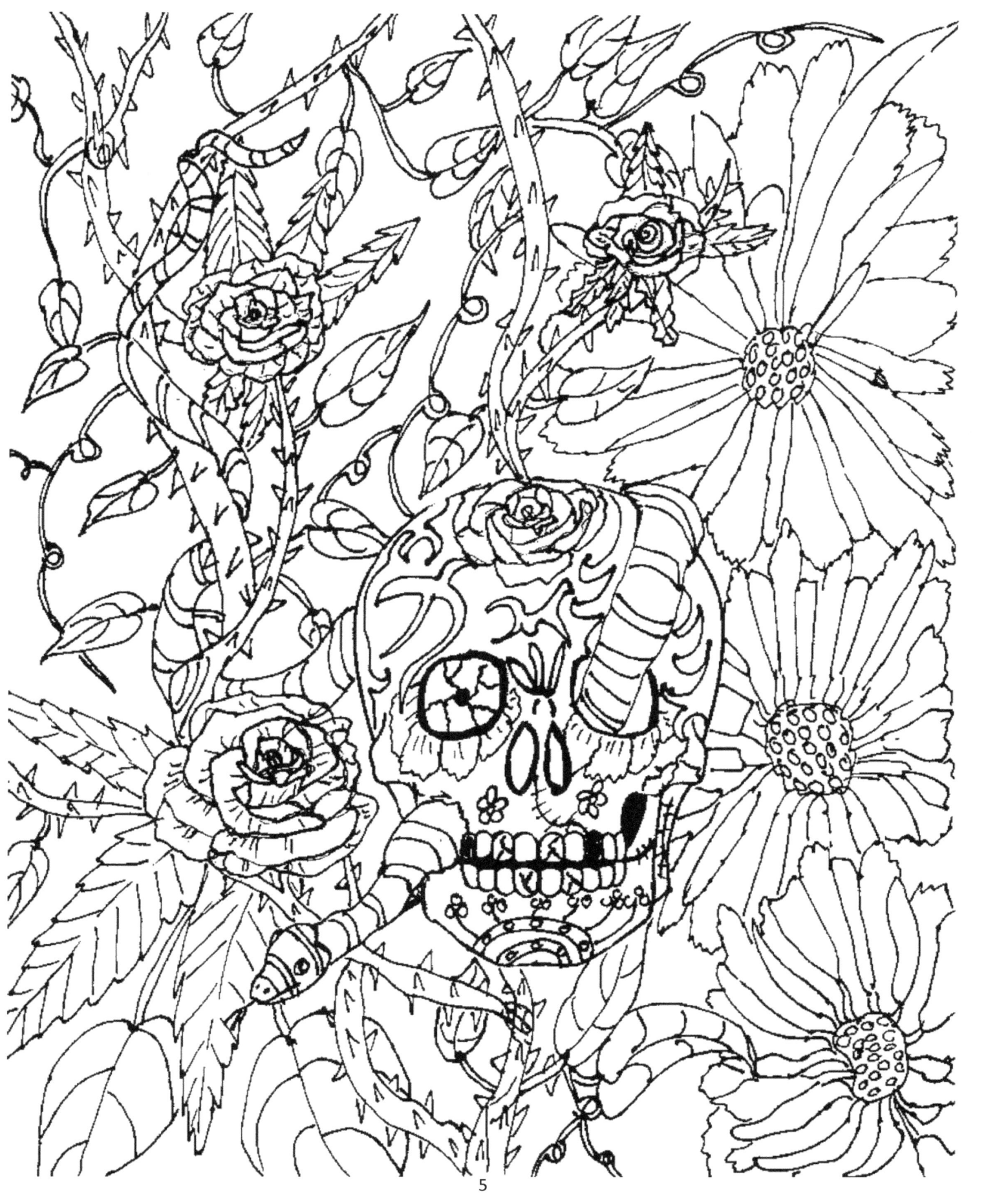

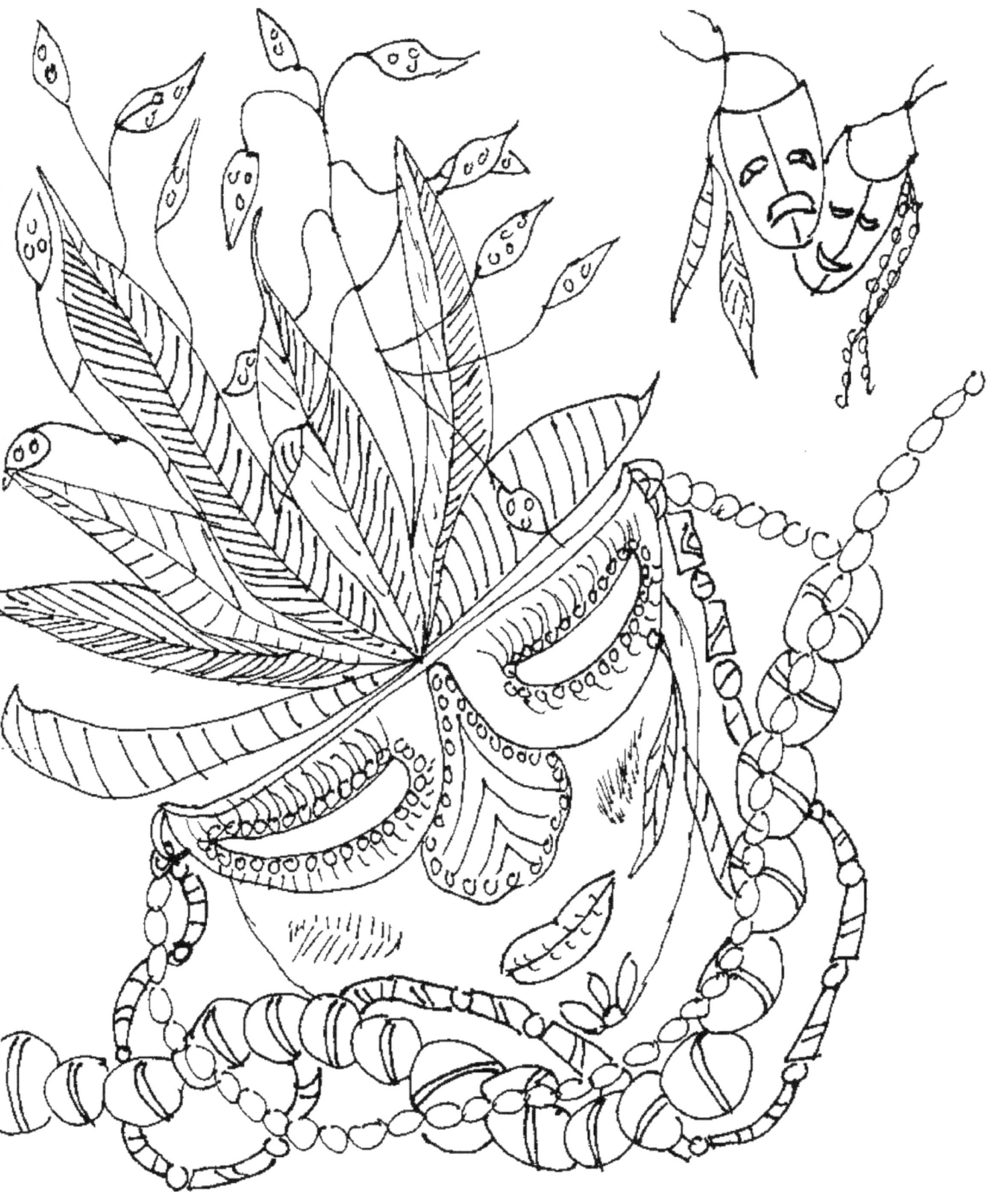

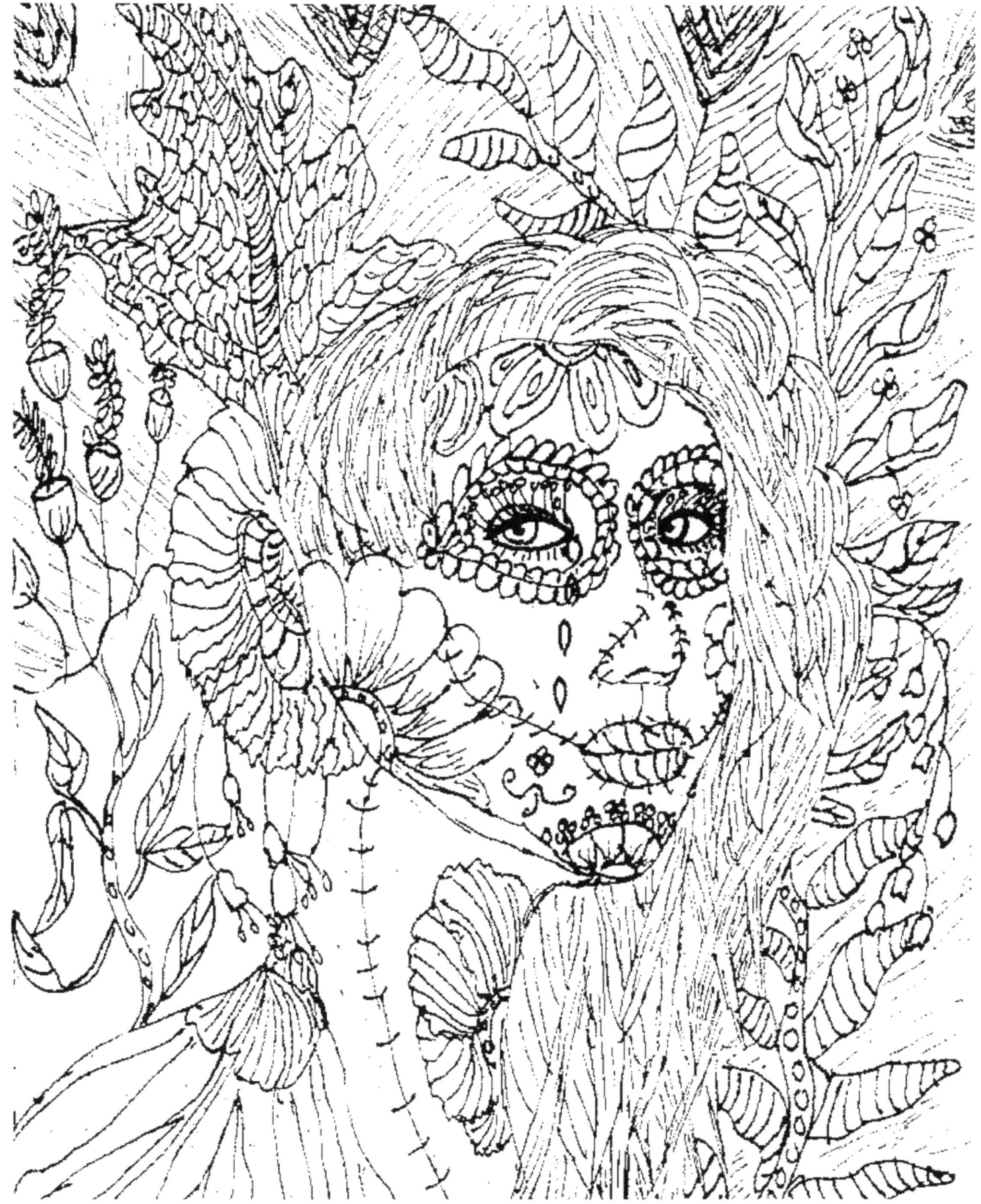

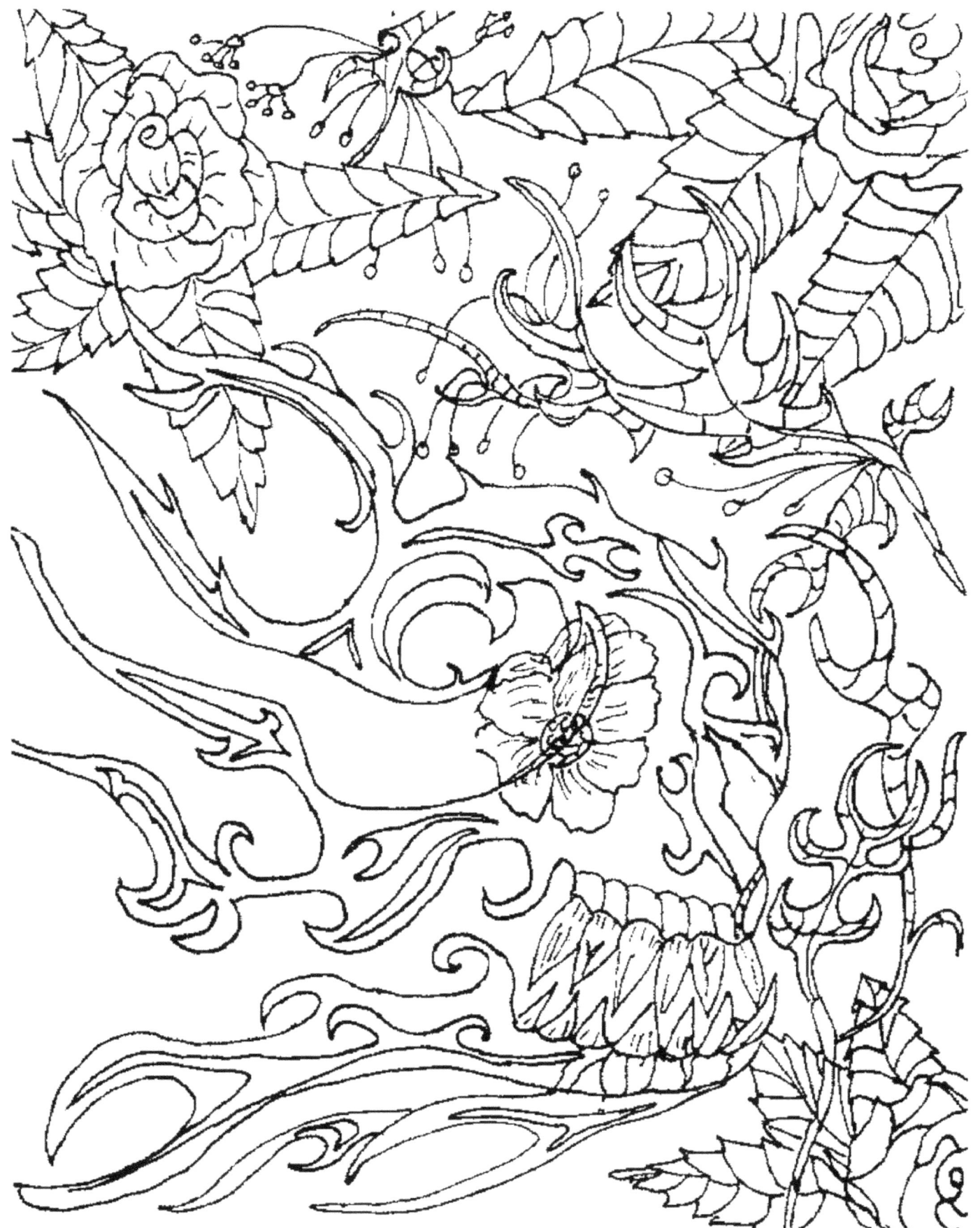

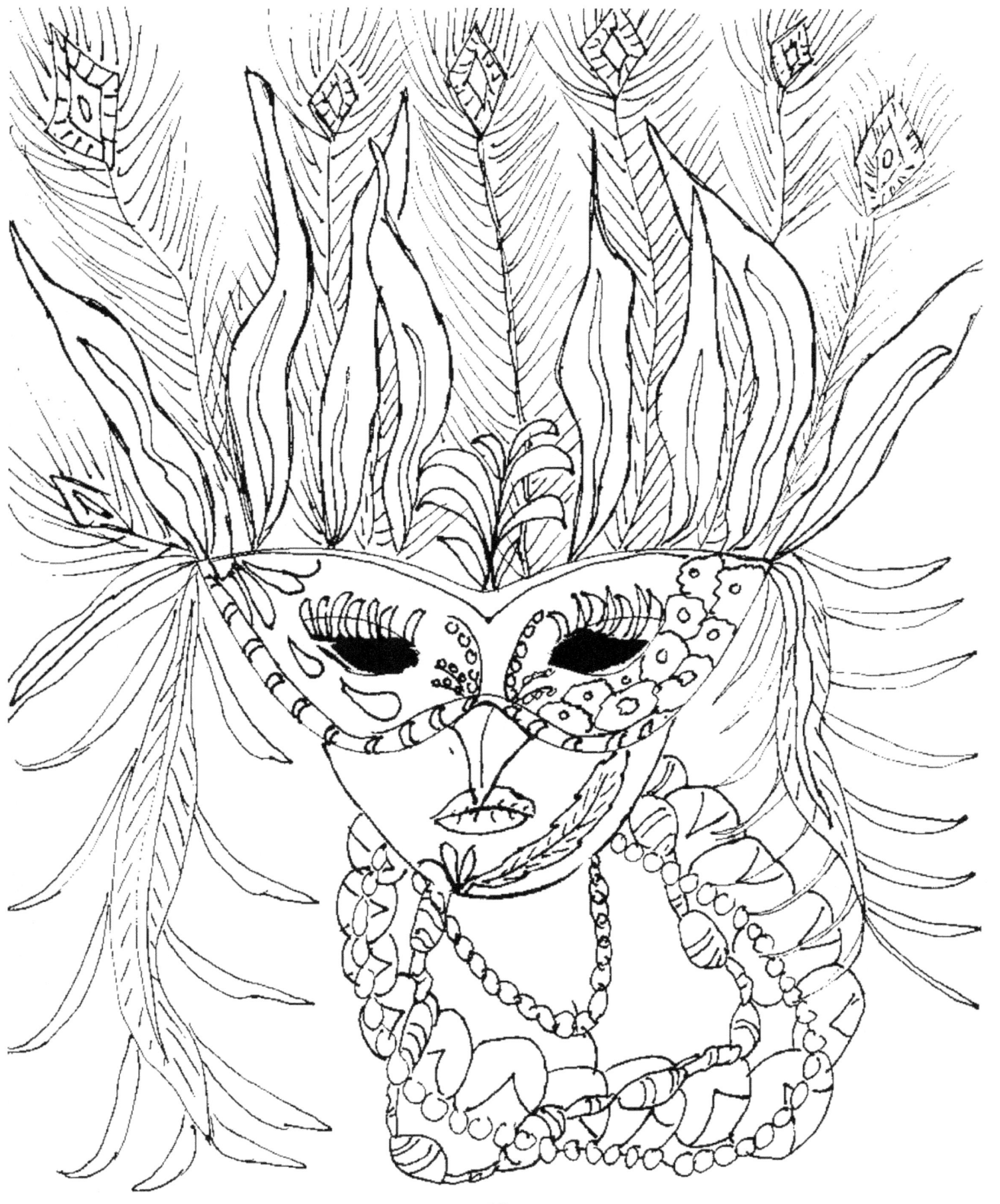

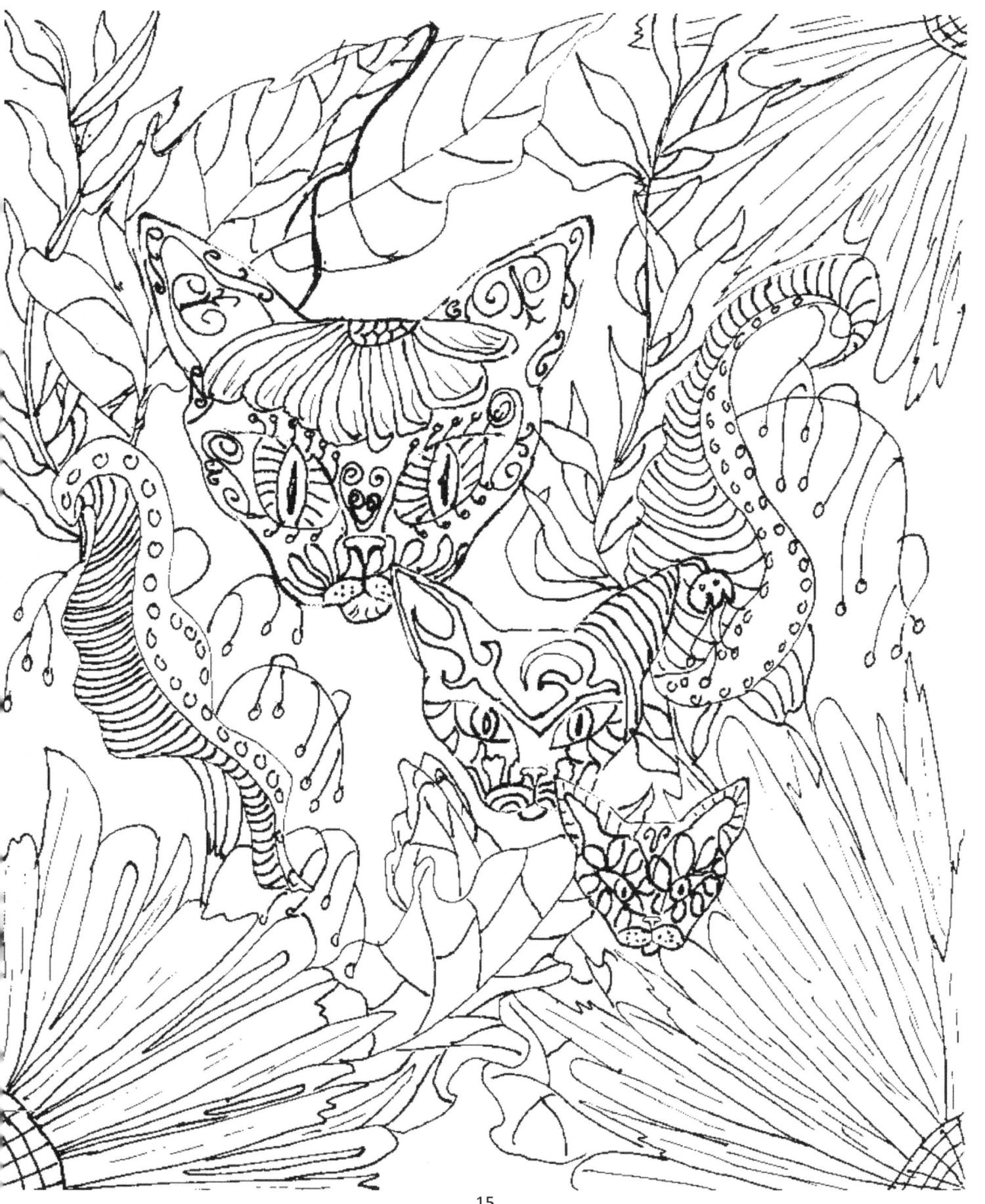

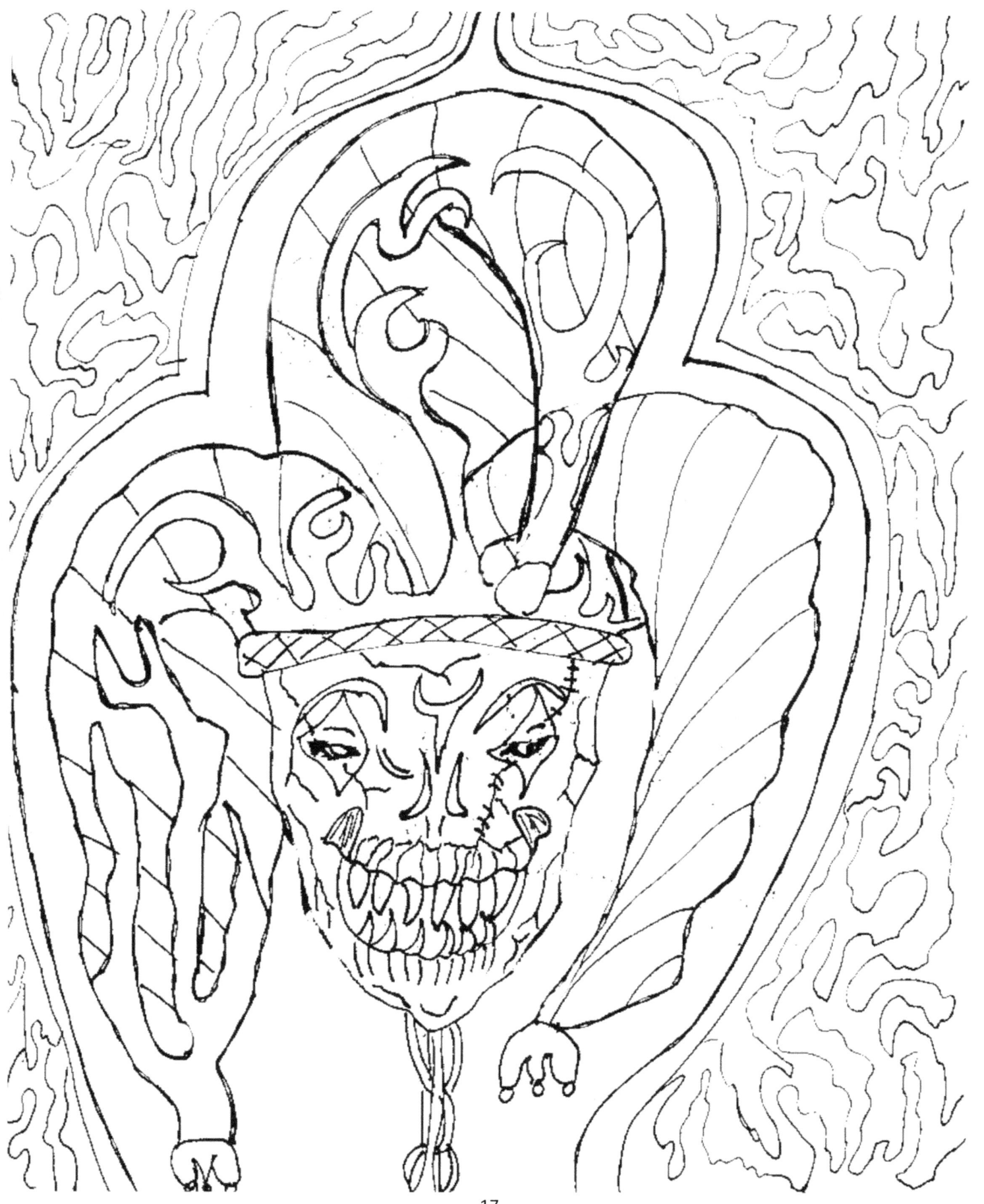

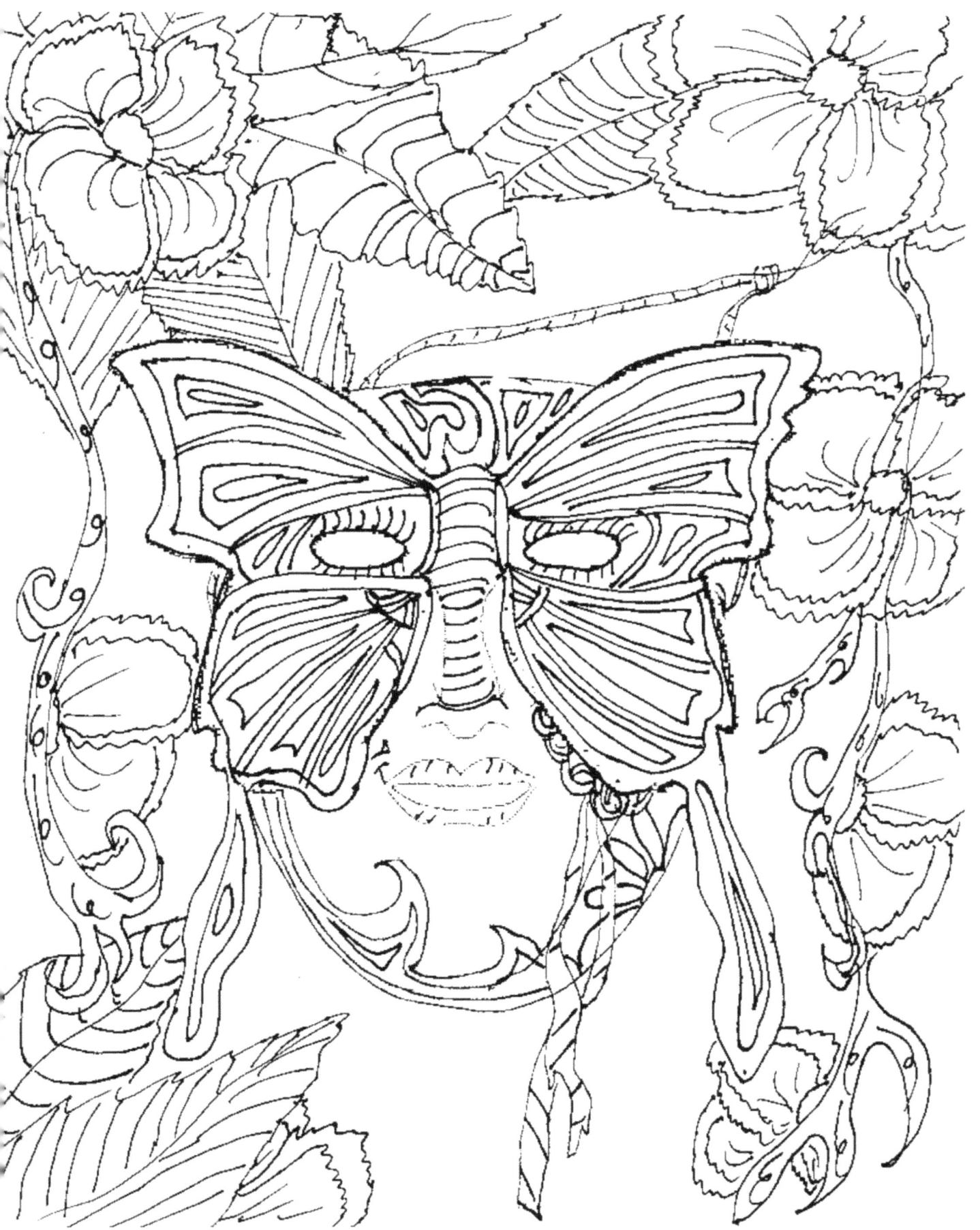

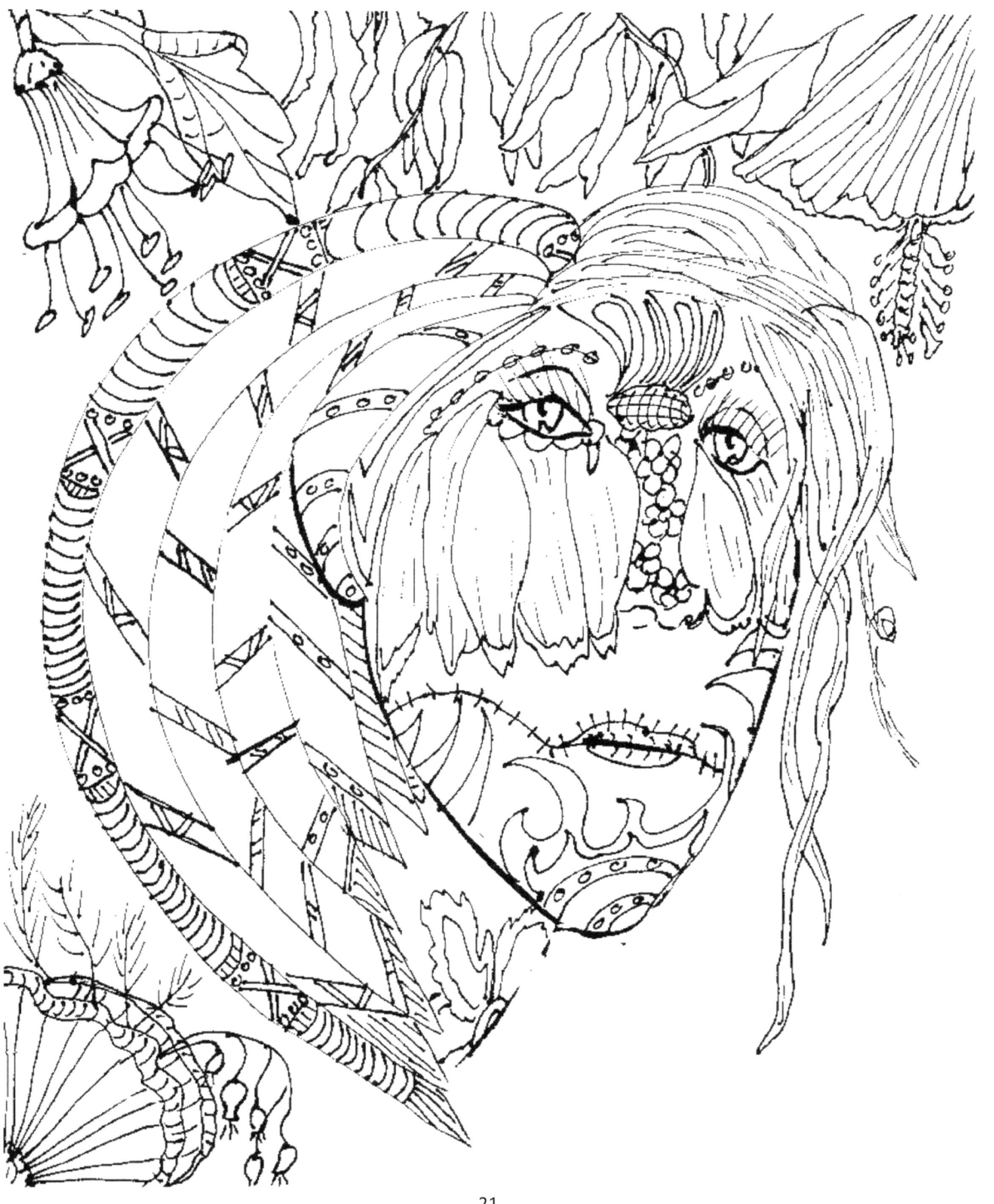

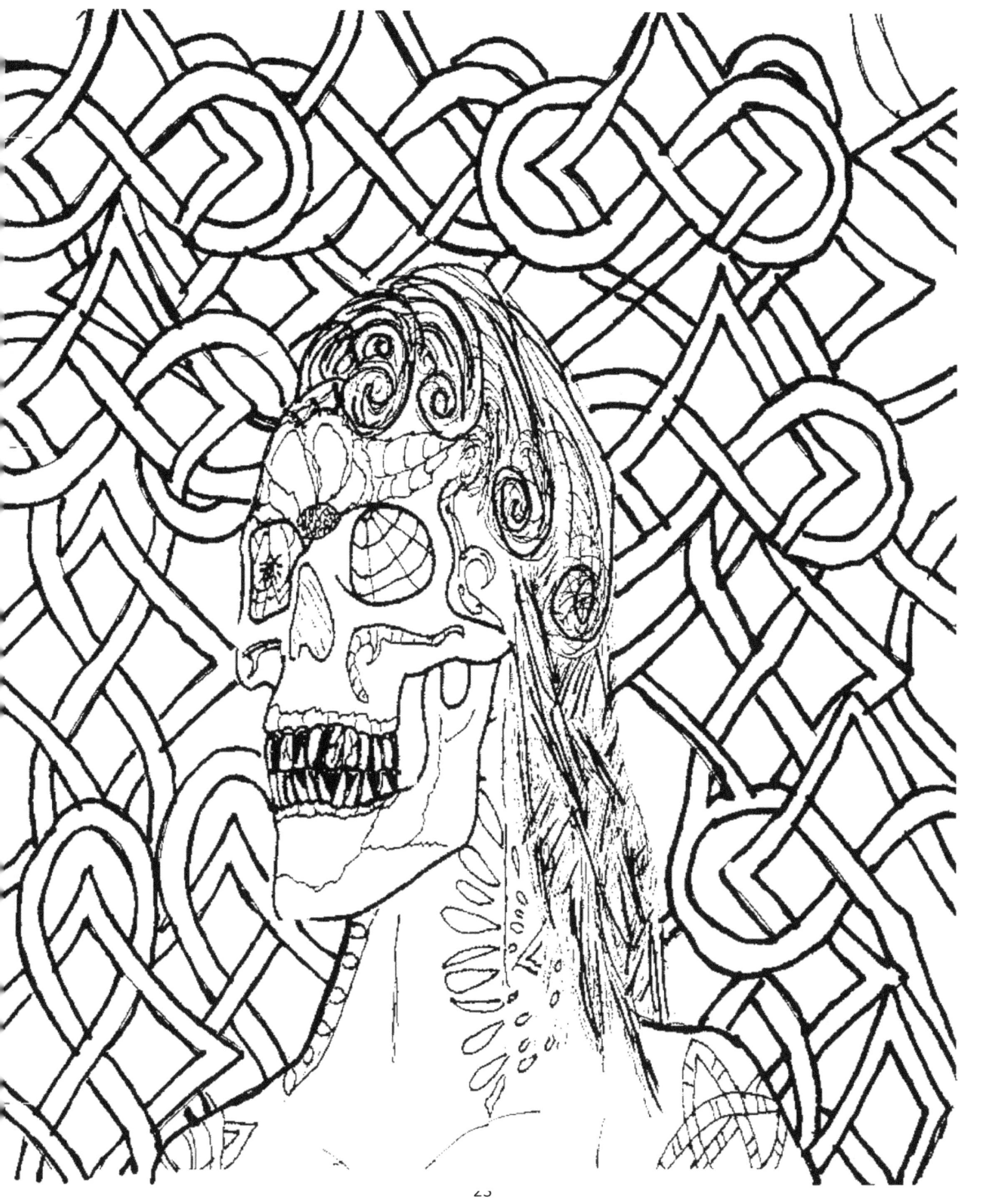

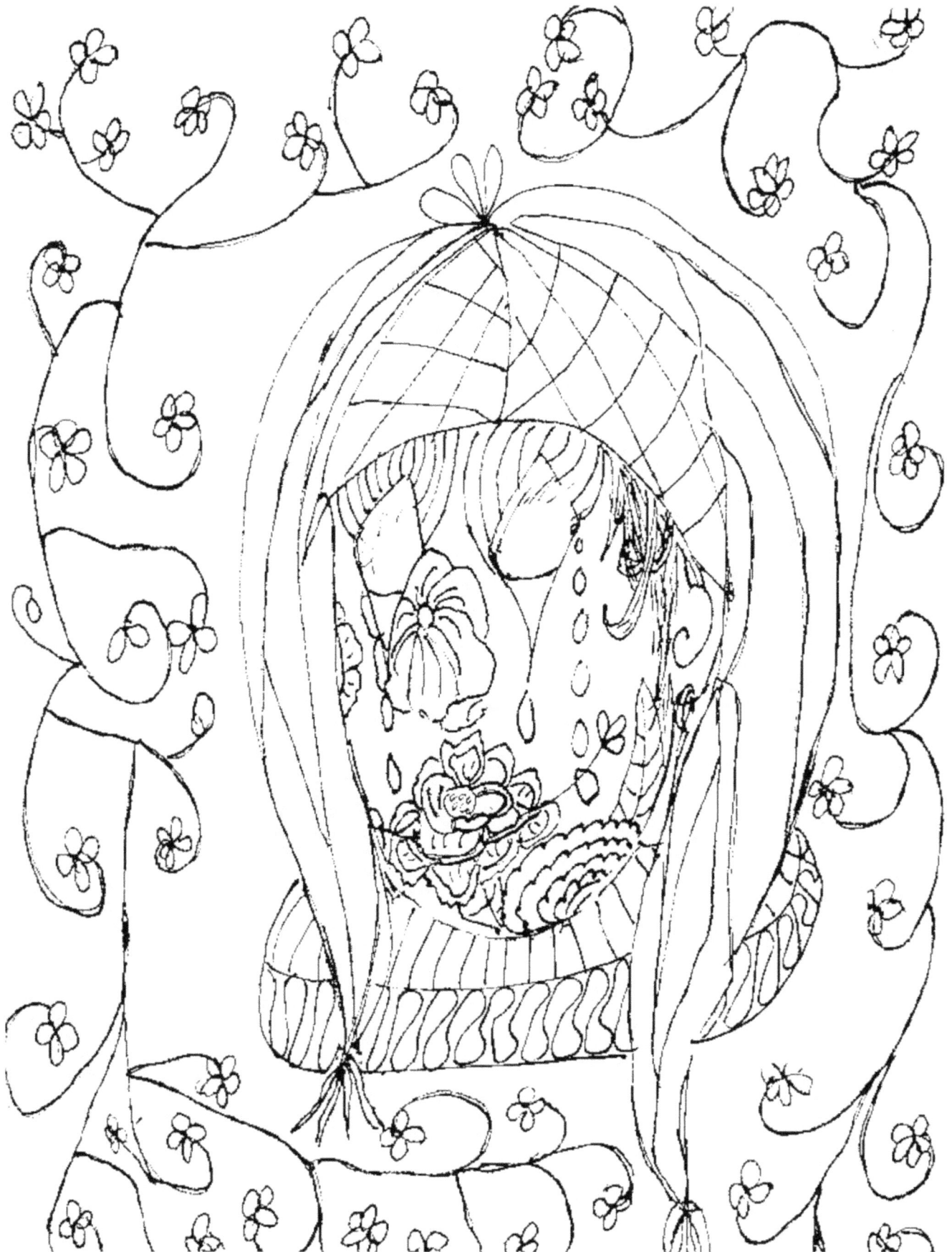

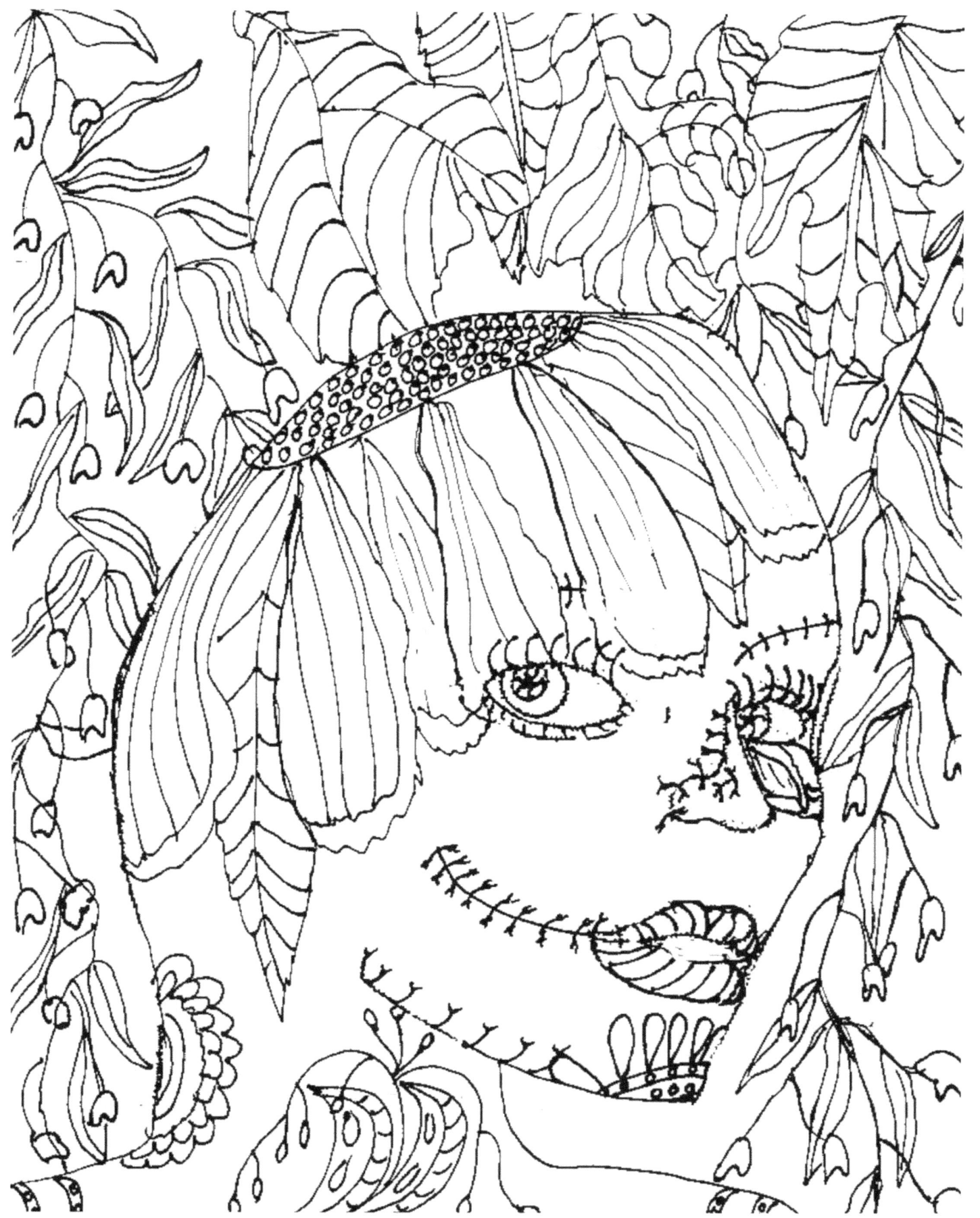

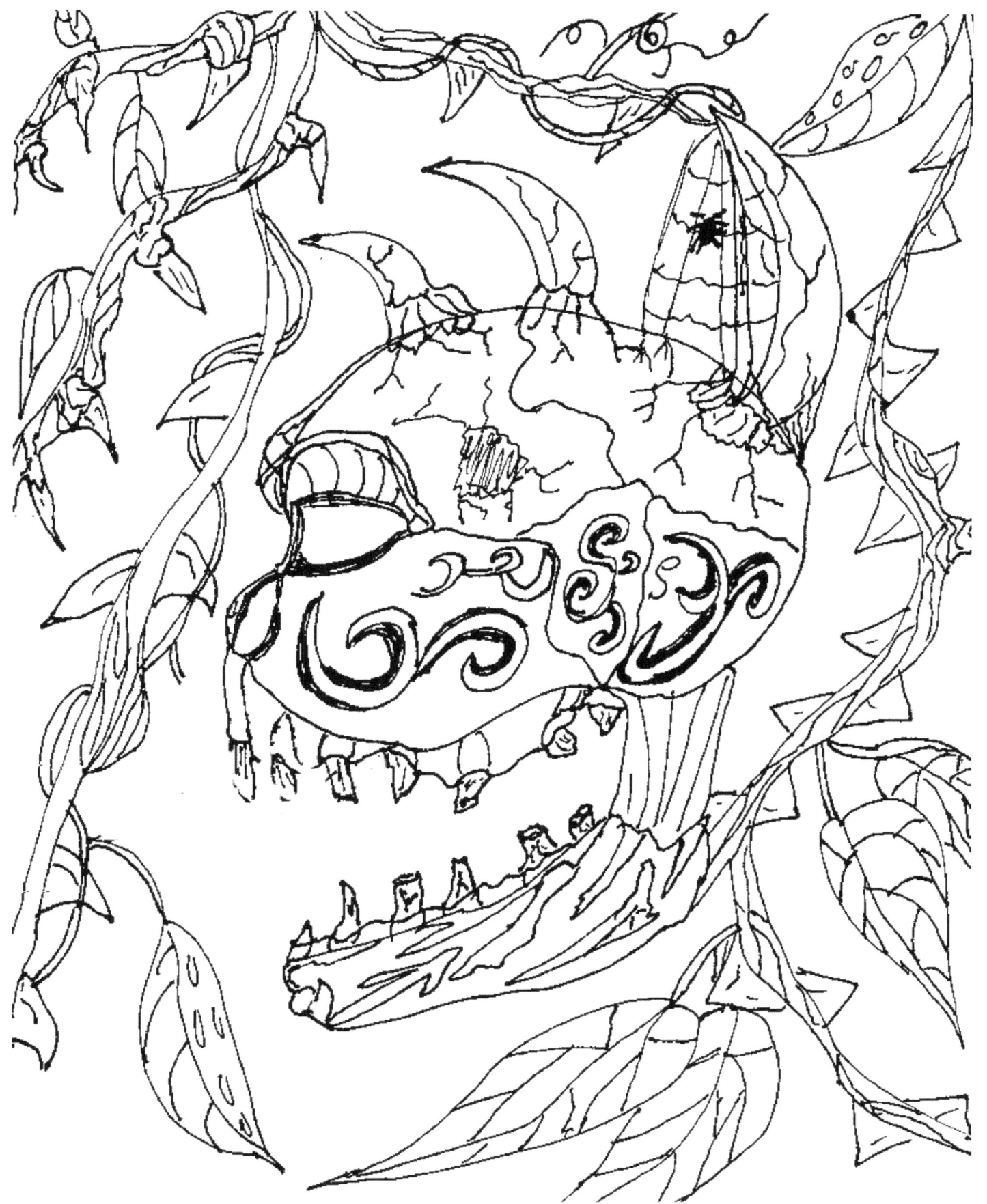

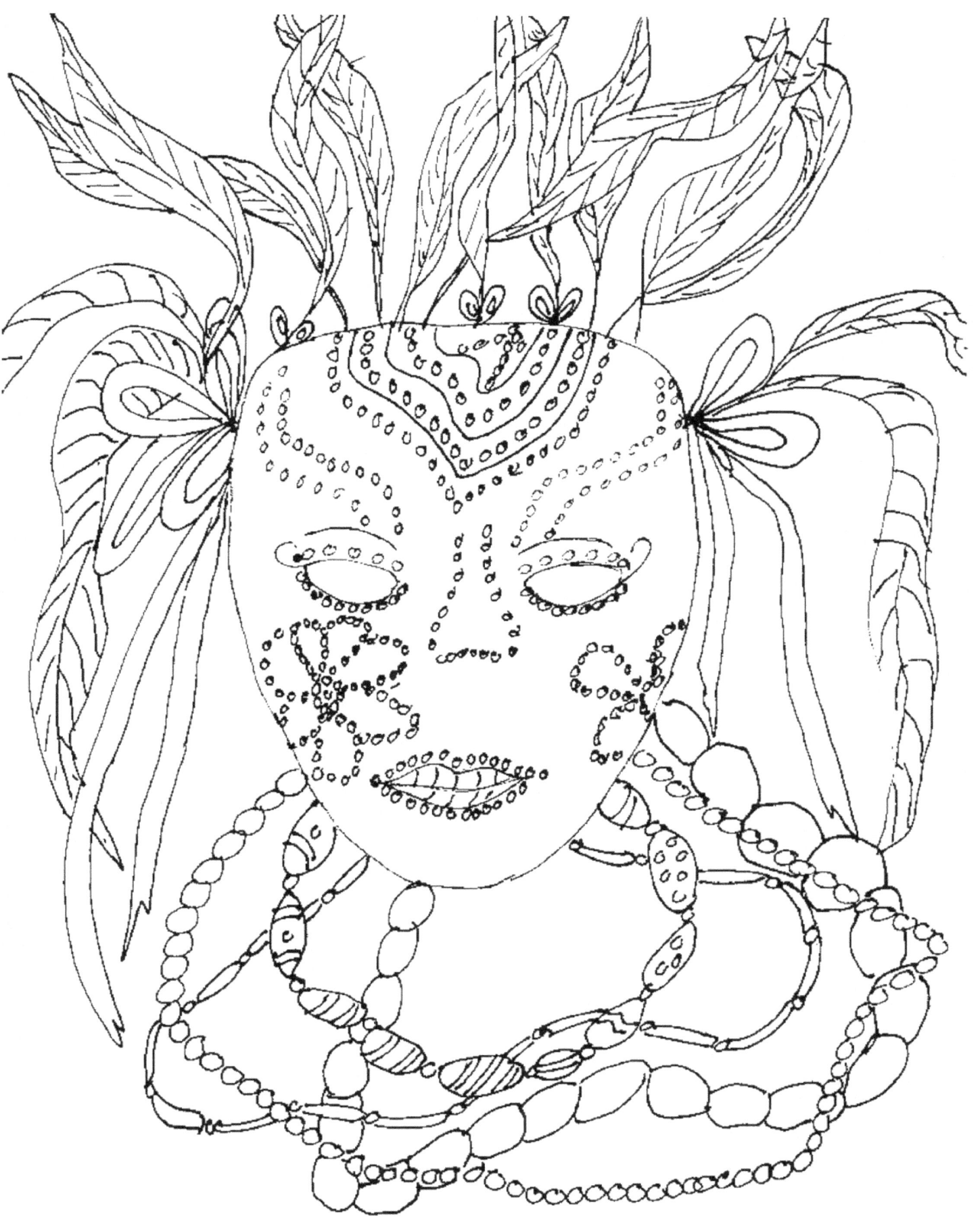

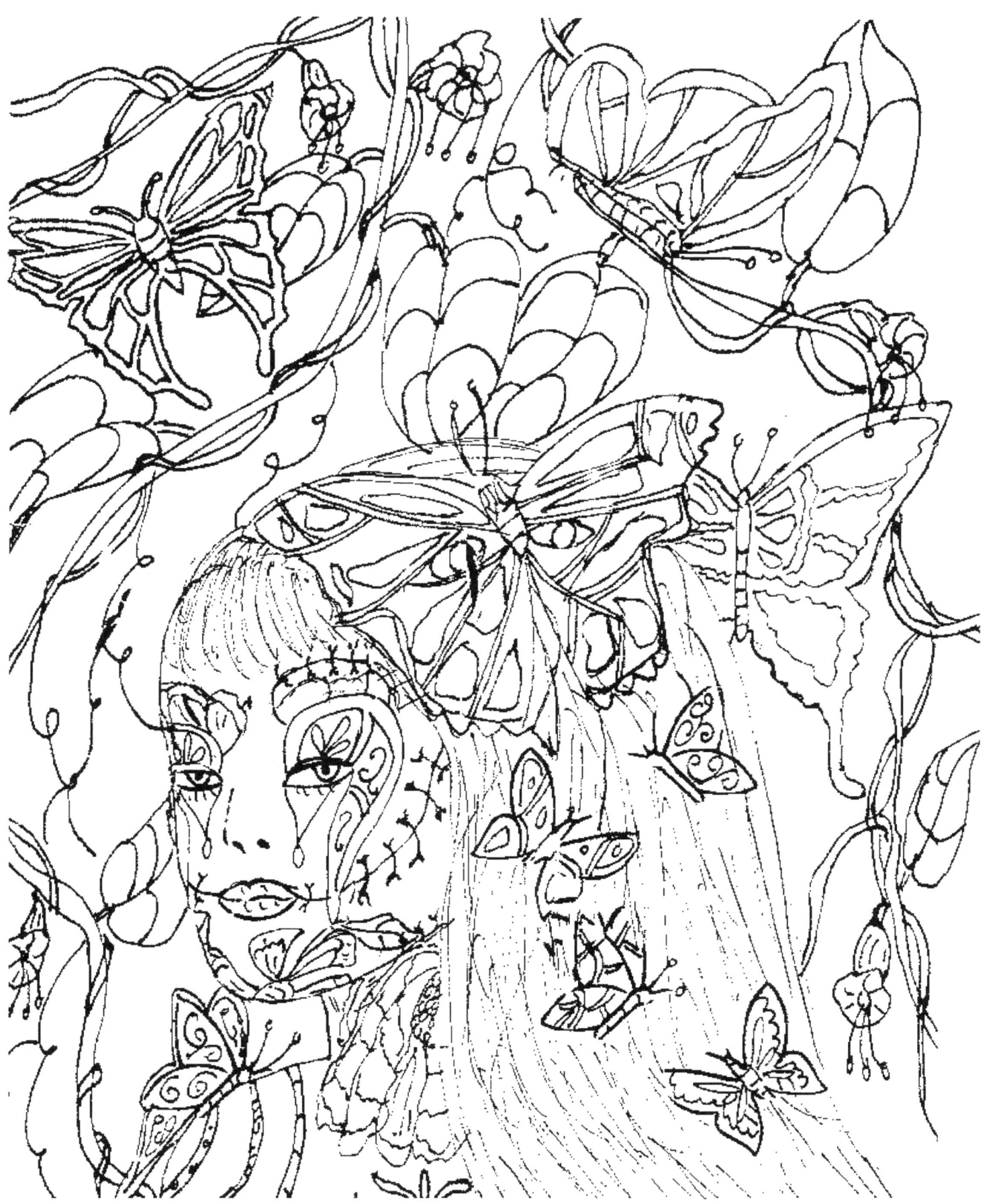

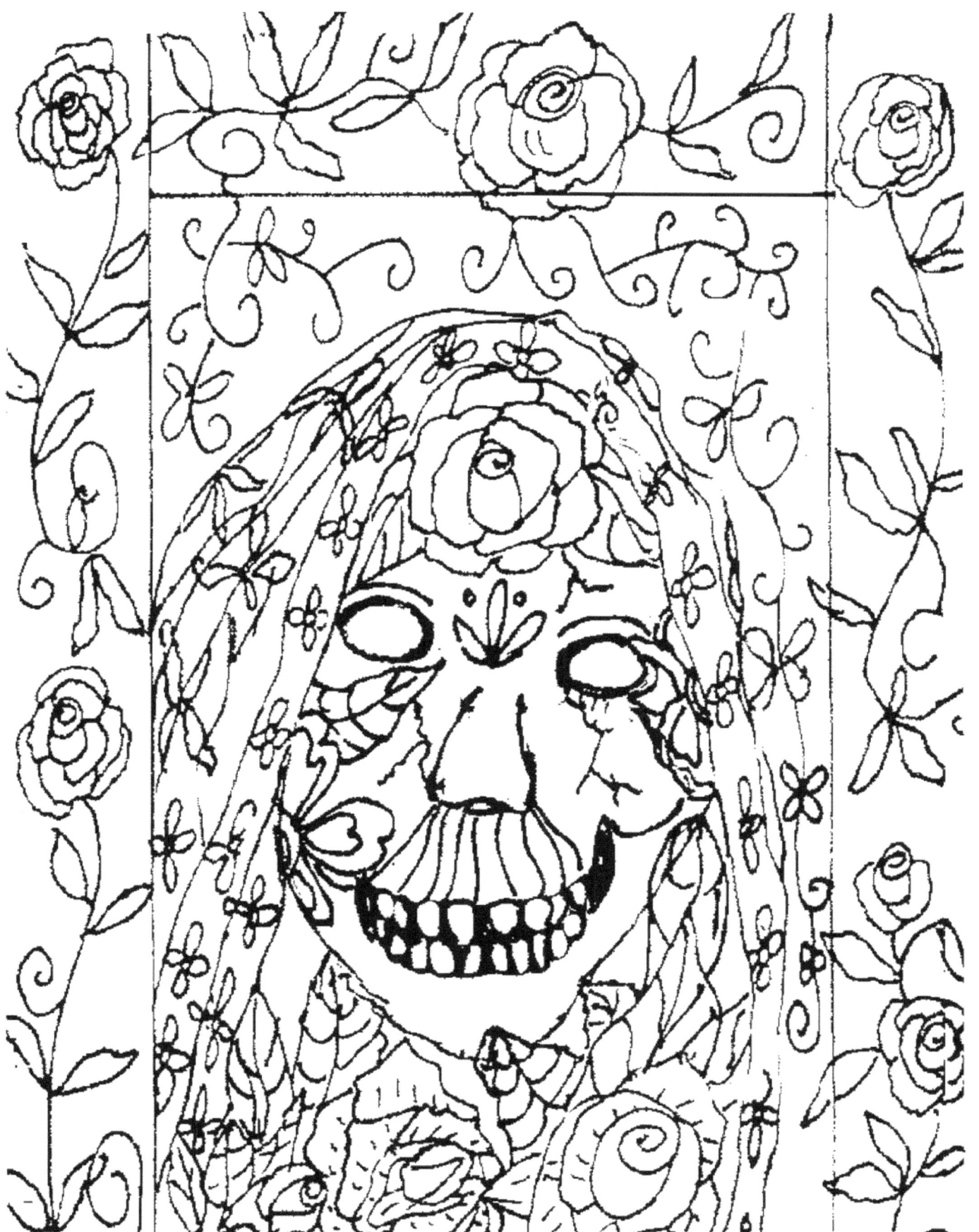

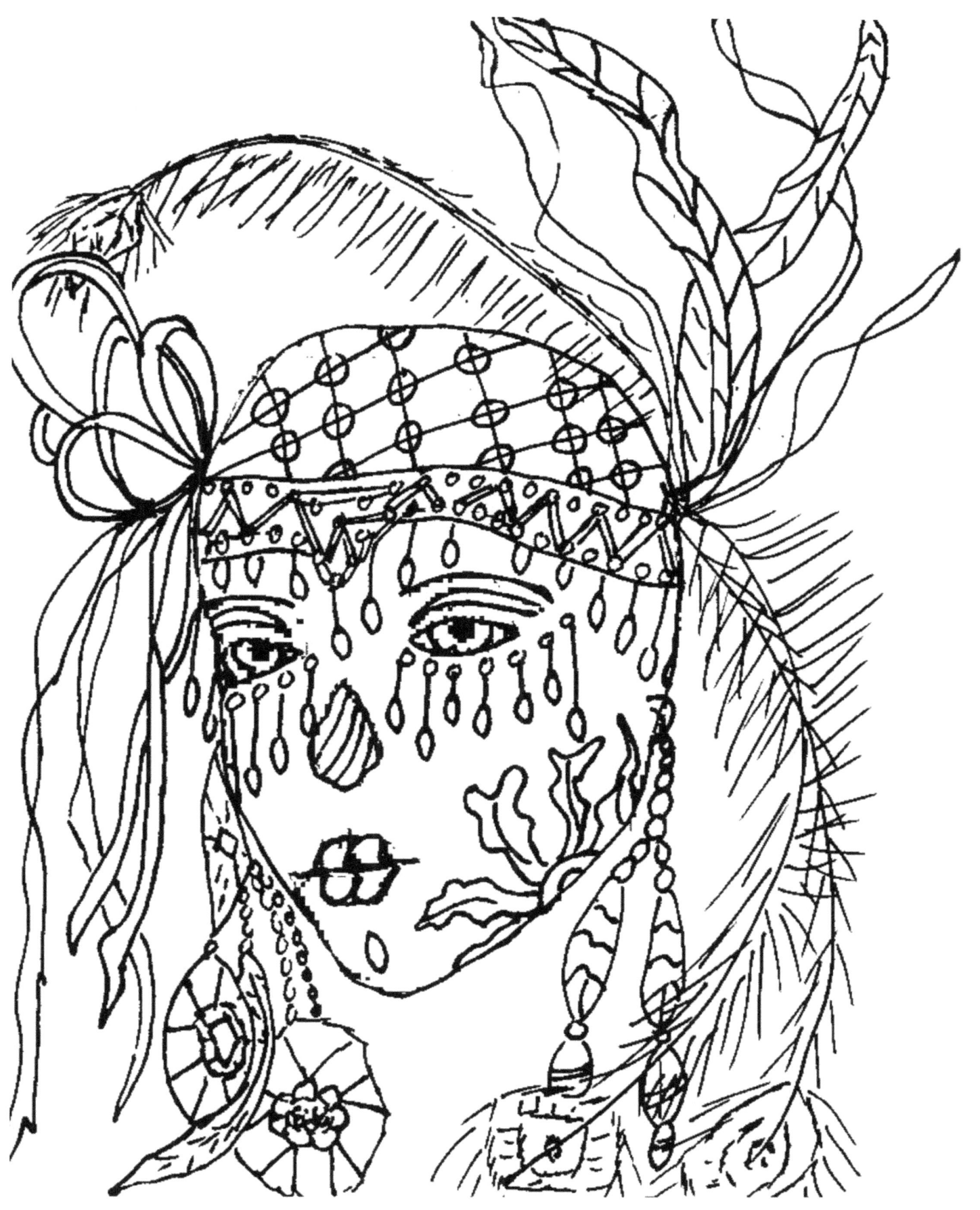

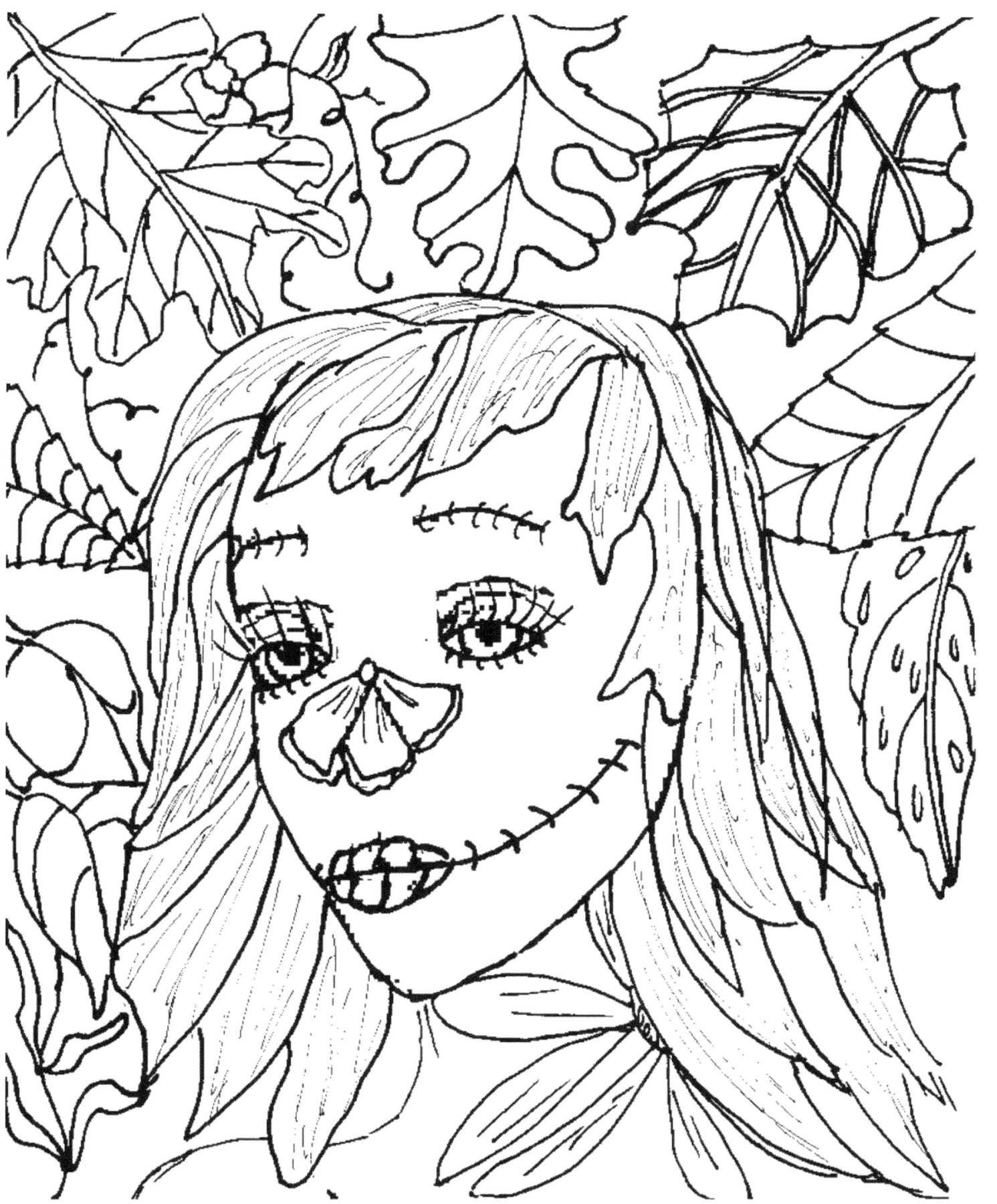

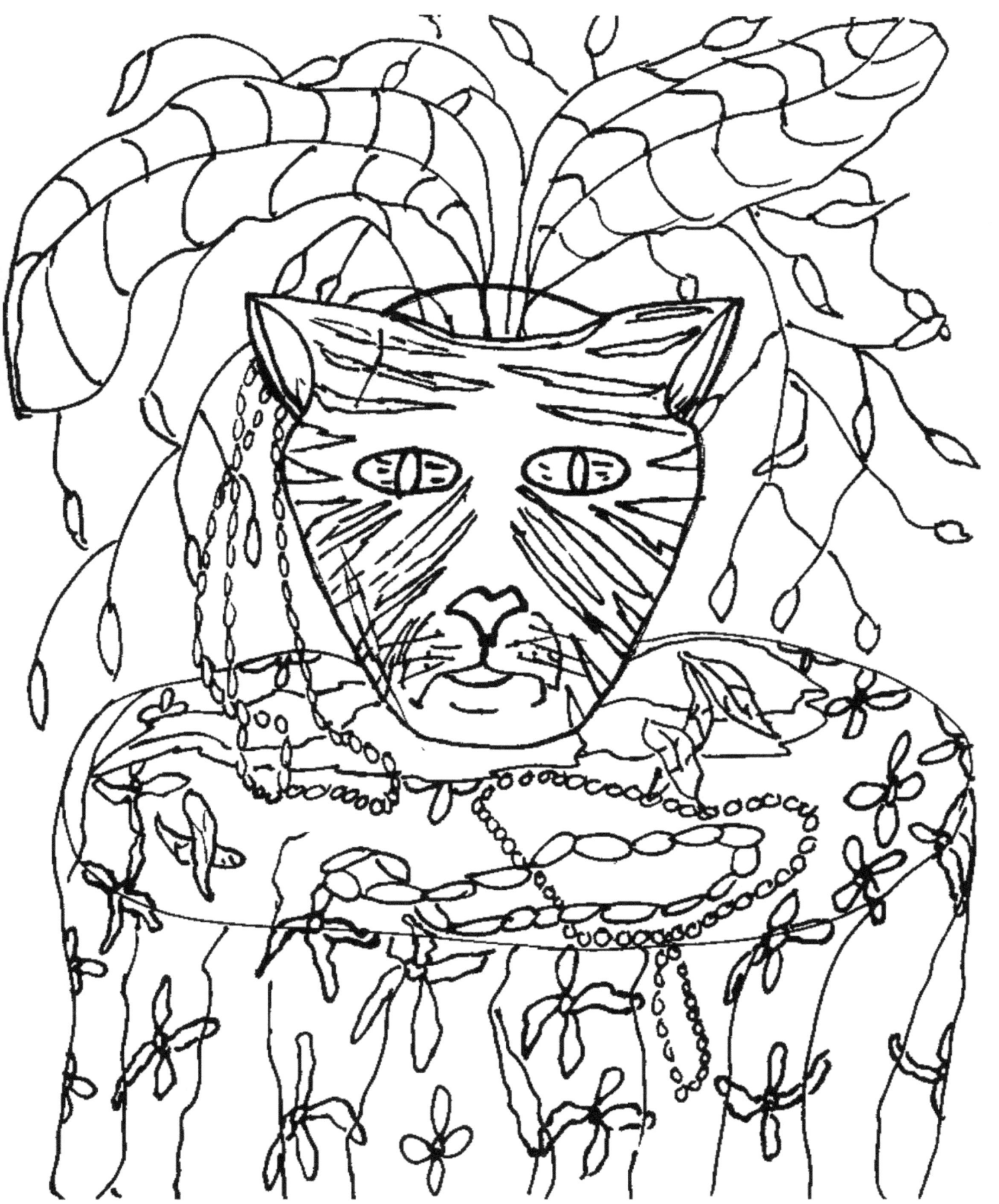

Thank you for choosing this coloring book and supporting an independent author/artist.

If you enjoy the book be sure to check out my other coloring books.

Vol. 1 Chickens

Vol. 2 South West & Floral Designs

Vol. 3 Day of the Dead & Mardi Gras

Vol. 4 Fantasy Castles & Dragons

Vol. 5 Exotic birds

Also for Variety puzzle fans I have

Hidden story & Variety puzzles

Hidden story word search Variety puzzles

Challenger Word Search & Sudoku Puzzles

Puzzle books are paperback

For Horror Suspense readers

E-book & paperback

Road to Carnage

Syeribus Vol 1, 2

Vampire Dolls

Lighter fun reading

Cat detective stories

On Amazon search under the name Boelz

Prepper magazine E-book only

If a paperback is desired over a kindle email for better price

Feathermeadows@gmail.com